COMING OUT OF THE CLOSET WORKBOOK

The Need for Women's Ministry in Such a Time as This

REVEREND SHIRLEY Y. COBB

Highly Favored Publishing™
BOWIE, MARYLAND

Coming Out of the Closet Workbook
Copyright © 2012 Shirley Cobb

Published by Highly Favored Publishing™
Bowie, MD 20716 USA
highlyfavoredpublishing@gmail.com
www.highlyfavoredpublishing.com
Highly Favored Publishing™ is an entity of Highly Favored, L.L.C.

ISBN: 978-0-9835157-5-3

No part of this publication may be reproduced, stored in a retrieval system, or transmitted, in any form, or by any means, electronic, mechanical, photocopying, recording, or otherwise, without the prior consent of the publisher.

All scripture quotations, unless otherwise indicated, are taken from the King James Version (KJV). Other scripture references are from the following sources: The Bible in Basic English (BBE), The Holy Bible, English Standard Version® (ESV®), copyright © 2001 by Crossway, a publishing ministry of Good News Publishers. Used by permission. All rights reserved. Holy Bible, New International Version® (NIV), copyright © 1973, 1978, 1984. Used by permission of Zondervan. All rights reserved.

Printed in the United States of America

Contents

Overview ... 5

Exercises

1. The Closet ... 7
2. The Invisible Child ... 13
3. Dead Woman Walking ... 19
4. Coming Out of the Closet ... 23
5. The Need for Ministry ... 27
6. Stages of a Woman ... 33
7. Who Am I? ... 39
8. He Came to Set the Captives Free ... 43
9. Life is Less Than Perfect ... 49
10. In the Beginning: The Making of Woman ... 57
11. Issues, Issues, Issues ... 63
12. Take Out the Trash & Throw Away the Garbage ... 71
13. Forgiveness ... 75
14. I Am Who God Says I Am ... 81
15. Hands ... 85

Notes ... 89

OVERVIEW

༄

This workbook is a companion to the book *Coming Out of the Closet: The Need for Women's Ministry in Such a Time as This* (2012). It is best utilized for group use, such as in a women's ministry class, support group, or book club. However, it can be used for individual study, as well. I encourage you to answer the questions and prompts honestly, but the choice is yours whether you share your responses and thoughts. As noted in the book, many times, the first step to healing and moving beyond our pain is to admit our pain. William Shakespeare wrote in *Macbeth*, "Give sorrow words, [for] the grief that does not speak whispers the o'er-fraught heart and bids it break." Begin to give words to your pain, your guilt, and your grief by answering the questions contained in this workbook.

I also encourage you to begin keeping a journal, if you do not already. Throughout the book are blank pages just for you to write. Write out your anger, your thoughts, and your sadness. Write out the feelings you have and chronicle them from the start of the book to the end. Answer the questions again months from now. Revisit your journal and writings and watch the progression of your feelings. Hopefully, that progression is toward healing and wholeness. However, if your thoughts are still filled with an overwhelming amount of anger and hurt at the conclusion of this workbook, or even while reading the book, I encourage you to seek spiritual guidance through a trusted spiritual leader or professional help.

Thank you so much for your support through the purchase of this companion workbook. I pray God will richly bless you as you begin the painful, yet purposeful, journey of coming out of your closet.

In His Service,

Shirley Y. Cobb

Exercise one

The Closet

> I realized that as long as he was allowed such control over my life, I would remain in that closet forever. I knew that as long as he was allowed the safe haven of that dark closet, I, and millions of women like me, would belong to him. I was not willing to concede a lifetime to his dominance. Therefore, with all the energy I could muster, I pushed open the door and did not just come out of the closet, but I ran toward The Light, The Light of Freedom!
>
> (from *Coming Out of the Closet*, Chapter Two)

Often, we do not realize that our closet experiences directly influence every decision we make (or do not make) and every relationship in which we involve ourselves. Even our personalities and behaviors are shaped by our closet experience(s). Therefore, we must identify the root, confront its ugliness, and seek healing. Doing so may drudge up unpleasant memories and feelings, so if it becomes too difficult, discuss it with your ministry leader or another trusted spiritual leader. You may also need to seek professional counseling. Many of us may have never shared our story, and sharing may be painful to do. However, in order to move toward healing and wholeness and to ultimately become free, we must share—not only for ourselves but for countless others who may benefit, as well. In the space provided, please share your own closet experience(s).

Exercise two
The invisible child

> Invisibility required silence, and silence required suppression, another costly prerequisite. That suppression was a total surrendering of my right to be heard or to confront my adversary. I know now what I did not know as a little girl or young woman: such a trade-off only built a prison that held me captive, captive to the desires and wishes of others who were all too willing to have their way with little or no regard for my wants or needs.
>
> (from Coming Out of the Closet, Chapter Three)

What has been shared with you by your parents or others about your life from conception until the day you were born? What were you told about your mother's pregnancy—her feelings, health, or state of mind—or the circumstances surrounding your birth?

_____
_____
_____
_____
_____
_____
_____
_____
_____
_____
_____
_____

Take a moment to go back in your mind as far as you can, to your earliest remembrance. Briefly describe these early experiences, whether positive or negative, and the impact they had on your life.

EARLIEST REMBRANCE:

_____
_____
_____
_____
_____
_____
_____
_____
_____
_____
_____
_____

Whether positive or negative, briefly describe your experiences during childhood and the impact these experiences had on your life.

CHILDHOOD YEARS (ages 2-12):

_____
_____
_____
_____
_____
_____
_____
_____
_____
_____
_____
_____
_____
_____

Whether positive or negative, briefly describe your experiences during adolescence and the impact these experiences had on your life.

ADOLESCENT YEARS (ages 13-17):

_____
_____
_____
_____
_____
_____
_____
_____
_____
_____
_____
_____
_____
_____
_____

Whether positive or negative, briefly describe your experiences during your young adult years and the impact these experiences had on your life.

YOUNG ADULT YEARS (ages 18-35):

_____
_____
_____
_____
_____
_____
_____
_____
_____
_____
_____
_____
_____
_____

Whether positive or negative, briefly describe your experiences during your adult years and the impact these experiences had on your life.

ADULT YEARS (ages 36-59):

_____
_____
_____
_____
_____
_____
_____
_____
_____
_____
_____
_____
_____
_____

Whether positive or negative, briefly describe your experiences during your senior adult years and the impact these experiences had on your life.

SENIOR ADULT YEARS (ages 60 & older):

_____
_____
_____
_____
_____
_____
_____
_____
_____
_____
_____
_____
_____
_____
_____

If you had positive experiences during a particular age period, describe how you would help someone approaching or already in this same period have a greater chance of having positive life experiences.

_____
_____
_____
_____
_____
_____
_____
_____
_____
_____
_____
_____
_____
_____
_____

For life experiences that were not positive, what are some things you wish you could have changed?

___

Why do you think these changes would have made a difference in your life?

___

Would you describe yourself as an "invisible child"? Why or why not?

___

Exercise three
Dead woman walking

I hid myself in plain sight of others. Every step I took was another step toward oblivion. I was not Yvonne. I was what the hands in the closet made me—a dead woman walking. My mental state was in such disarray that I perceived the executioner (the hands) not as a dreaded foe but rather a dear friend, for he possessed the power, by mere confession, to free me from the prison in which I resided.

(from *Coming Out of the Closet*, Chapter Four)

Because of our closet experiences, many of us do not realize that although we are alive, we are not living. We get up, go about our daily tasks, eat, sleep, and do it all over again the next day. Some of us grew from little girls to teenagers to adult women, never really having experienced the abundant life God intended for us to have.

1. In your own words, how do you define a "dead woman walking"?

_____
_____
_____
_____

2. Do you feel you are or ever have been a dead woman walking? If so, explain why and note what events made you feel this way?

_____
_____
_____
_____

If you do not, explain why.

_____
_____
_____
_____

Do you recall an association with someone you felt met your definition of a dead woman walking? Why did they meet your definition?

_____
_____
_____
_____

3. Psalm 30:5 promises, "Weeping may endure for a night, but joy cometh in the morning." How long was your journey to freedom?

_____
_____
_____

4. What helped you break out of or rise above the situation and become free?

_____
_____
_____
_____

5. If you are not free, how long have you been walking in chains?

_____
_____
_____
_____

6. What do you feel will help you become free?

_____
_____
_____
_____

Exercise four
Coming out of the closet

As women, we must come out of the closet in order to experience a physical, emotional, psychological, and most importantly, a spiritual metamorphosis. We must come out of the closet and journey from the darkness and loneliness of a cocoon in order to come into The Light, Jesus Christ, and take flight as the beautiful, fluttering butterfly that God designed us to be.

(from *Coming Out of the Closet*, Chapter Five)

At this point, you have shared your closet experience(s). This lesson is designed to reveal how those closet experiences directly or indirectly affect every area of our lives. Remember: freedom begins with a decision—the decision to be made whole. Until we come out of the closet, freedom can never be experienced in the fullest.

1. In your own words, how do you define "closet"?

_____
_____
_____
_____

2. What or who *has been* your closet?

_____
_____
_____
_____

3. What or who *is* your closet?

_____
_____
_____
_____
_____
_____
_____
_____

4. What feelings or thoughts do you associate with your closet?

_____
_____
_____
_____

5. Do you feel you are still in a closet? Explain.

_____
_____

_____
_____

6. What do you feel you need in order to help you come out of the closet?
_____
_____
_____
_____

Exercise five
The need for ministry

Women's ministry is an avenue that helps women learn how to cope with their issues while they are going through them, learn why women are more predisposed to certain issues and what God's Word says about these issues, and learn how to apply the principles of God's Word in their lives to help bring about a resolution. Fellowship is not ministry. Ministry is ongoing with some degree of regularity and is structured to create the life-altering experience that is needed for deliverance.

(from *Coming Out of the Closet*, Chapter Six)

In order to begin the process of coming out of our closets and moving toward the freedom that coming out can bring, it takes active involvement in ministry. The experiences that some of us have been through cannot be adequately addressed in a quick-fix, one-time setting. It requires more. Once you have made the decision to become whole, make certain you do whatever is spiritually necessary to achieve this desired and deserved goal.

1. Ministry and fellowship. How do you define each?

   a) Ministry: _____
   _____
   _____
   _____
   _____
   _____
   _____

   b) Fellowship: _____
   _____
   _____
   _____
   _____
   _____
   _____

2. Do you feel women in your church seek ministry or avoid it? Explain.
   _____
   _____
   _____
   _____
   _____
   _____

3. What needs do you see for the women of your church (all ages)? (Define the needs by age groups, if desired.)
   _____
   _____
   _____
   _____

The Purpose of Ministry

Helps women who have been damaged physically, emotionally, morally, and spiritually move toward wholeness

Empowers women to rise out of feelings of hopelessness & despair

Addresses strongholds from the past so women can start living in the present in order to have a successful future

Lifts women who suffer from low self-esteem and depression as a result of their victimization by society

Inspires women to excel in their homes, work places, and places of worship as they realize they are no longer victims but victors in Christ

Nourishes and strengthens relationships among women and helps women feel better about themselves, moving them toward wholeness, therefore creating stronger membership and greater support of the leader's vision in churches and other organizations

Guides women to higher levels of spiritual growth through God's Word

4. How do you define "Woman"?

_____
_____
_____
_____

5. What is she?

_____
_____
_____
_____

6. Who taught you what you know today about being a woman?

_____
_____
_____
_____

7. What do you wish you had known about womanhood earlier in life? Why?

_____
_____
_____
_____

8. What makes woman uniquely female (not just a different version of the male)?

_____
_____
_____
_____
_____
_____

Exercise six
STAGES OF A WOMAN

> It is important to understand that with the exception of the creational woman and the young woman, the rest of these stages may not occur necessarily in this order. We may be chronologically past a particular stage, but if we do not address certain problems that occurred during that stage, we can be mentally, emotionally, and spiritually in limbo and unable to embrace all the next stage has to offer.

(from *Coming Out of the Closet*, Chapter Seven)

In Cynthia Hicks' book *The Feminine Journey: Understanding the Biblical Stages of a Woman's Life*,[1] she identifies six life stages. For this lesson, go back as far as you can remember in your childhood, and discuss your memories and thoughts about each stage.

1. **The Creational Woman:** This stage ranges from puberty (approximately age 12) to age 18. What do you remember?

_____
_____
_____
_____
_____
_____
_____
_____
_____
_____
_____
_____
_____

2. **The Young Woman:** This stage generally ranges from age 18 to age 30. What do you remember?

_____
_____
_____
_____
_____
_____
_____
_____
_____
_____
_____
_____
_____

3. **The Nurturing Woman:** This stage may overlap with **The Young Woman**. In this stage, a woman embraces the pains and joys of motherhood. What do you remember? (Nurturing does not only apply to women who have actually given birth. We as women are nurturers by nature, so describe your nurturing experiences.)

___

4. **The Relational Woman:** In this stage, a woman celebrates rather than denigrates gender differences. She appreciates the fact that men are men and women are women. What do you remember? What are your thoughts?

___

5. **The Wounded Woman:** Wounded women are generally women who are divorced or widowed, or women who have been victimized by childhood trauma. How have you been wounded?

___

6. **The Woman of Strength:** In this stage, a woman is approaching the end of her journey. She is a teacher of wisdom and is akin to the Titus 2 woman who teaches the younger women how to be chaste and discreet. What do you remember?

___

7. Where do you feel your greatest strength lies?

___

8. What do you feel you still need to learn or know?

_____
_____
_____
_____

Exercise seven
WHO AM I?

    I wake up morning after morning, and I look in the mirror as I prepare for the day. There are some mornings when I look at the person looking back at me and say, *"I am woman . . . hear me roar! I am confident, compassionate, and content with my life and myself."* Then, there are other days when I look into the eyes of that person who is staring back at me and ask, *"Who are you, and what do you want from me?"*

(from *Coming Out of the Closet*, Chapter Seven)

Outside of knowing our name, many of us do not know who we truly are, and we may have a difficult time describing ourselves to others. Write in your own words **who you believe you are**. There is no page minimum. (If you are doing this lesson as part of a ministry class, be prepared to share with your group only what you are comfortable sharing.)

Exercise eight

He came to set the captives free

౮ No matter how "bad" you think you may be, no matter how "dirty" you may think you are, no matter how "crazy" people may think you are or if you feel you are losing your mind, no matter how many times you have been told you are nothing and no one wants you, no matter what habit you may have had or are still struggling with, Jesus said, "*Come unto me*." Even if you are still drinking, using drugs, prostituting yourself, or in an adulterous affair, just "*Come unto me*" (Matthew 11:28)!

(from *Coming Out of the Closet*, Chapter Eight)

As women, some of us remain spiritually dead because of those things that continue to hold us captive. We are in bondage and may not even realize it. We must know that Jesus came to free us from these things that bind us.

> The Spirit of the Lord is on me, because I am marked out by him to give good news to the poor; he has sent me to make well those who are broken-hearted; to say that the prisoners will be let go, and the blind will see, and to make the wounded free from their chains, To give knowledge that the year of the Lord's good pleasure is come. (Bible in Basic English, Luke 4:18-19)

Once we become a child of God, this mission becomes our mission. The "me" becomes "you" whom the Spirit should be upon. Therefore, it becomes our responsibility to do these things. Once we accept Jesus as our personal Savior, we can break down this passage and put it into the proper perspective. Then, we can answer these questions:

1. Since everyone is not called to preach in the traditional sense, from the pulpit, how do you fulfill this mission?

___

2. Who are the poor?

___

3. Who are the brokenhearted?

___

4. Who are the captives?

___

5. Whose sight needs to be recovered?

6. Who needs liberty?

7. What does it mean to be bruised?

8. What does the acceptable year of the Lord mean?

9. In your own words, define freedom.

10. Are you free as it relates to salvation? If so, tell your testimony.

THE DISPENSATION OF GRACE WAS USHERED IN AT CALVARY. JESUS BECAME THE:

Grave robber (who)

Redeemed us (and now)

Accepts us for who we are

Cancelled the penalty of sin (and offers us)

Eternal life

If you are not sure you are saved or have never accepted Christ as your personal Savior, read St. John 3:16 and Romans 10:9. Acknowledge that you are a sinner and in need of God's grace and forgiveness, and ask Christ to come into your heart.

(a) Confess with your mouth.
(b) Believe in your heart that Jesus is the Son of God.
(c) Believe that Jesus was raised from the dead.

AND THOU SHALT BE SAVED!

EXERCISE NINE

LIFE IS LESS THAN PERFECT

When we look back over our lives, like Abigail, many of us could agree that it was some kind of trouble that drove us to the Lord. Because we know we will have trouble, what is most crucial is the attitude we choose to have while we are going through our trouble. Even though life is less than perfect in some areas, we must stand so God gets the glory. We must not go our own way but remember to *"stand firm, hold your position, and see the salvation of the Lord on your behalf"* (2 Chronicles 20:17, ESV).

(from *Coming Out of the Closet*, Chapter Nine)

The Women's Movement

Cautious, careful people, always casting about to preserve the reputation and social standing, never can bring about a reform. Those who are really in earnest must be willing to be anything or nothing in the world's estimation, and publicly and privately, in season and out, avow their sympathy with despised and persecuted ideas and their advocates, and bear the consequences.[2]

1. What do you know about the leaders of the Women's Suffrage movement? During what time period did this movement occur?

2. Who was Lucretia Mott?

3. Who was Susan B. Anthony?

4. Who was Frances Willard?

5. Who was the first president of N.W.S.A. (The National Woman Suffrage Association)? In what year was this association formed?

6. Who was Lucy Stone?

7. Who was Elizabeth Cady Stanton?

8. Which president's wife, in 1777, asked her husband to "remember the ladies" when he and the Continental Congress began writing the laws for the new country? She said: "If particular care and attention is not paid to the ladies . . . we will not hold ourselves bound by any laws in which we have no voice or representation."[3]

9. When did women receive the right to vote?

10. Which amendment provided this right?

11. What person or organization was instrumental in helping to get this vote passed?

12. Who was Sojourner Truth, and why is she considered a pioneer for women's rights?

13. Who was the first woman elected to Congress, and in what year was she elected?
_____
_____
_____

14. Who was the first African American congresswoman, and in what year was she elected?
_____
_____
_____

15. Who was the first African American female millionaire?
_____
_____
_____

16. Who was the first African American female bishop?
_____
_____
_____

17. Who was the first African American First Lady in the White House and in what year?
_____
_____
_____

In 2008, we had for the first time in history a woman, Hilary Clinton, and an African American man, Barack Obama, as the democratic candidates for president of the United States of America. The first African American female president could be reading this book right now. Is it you? As women, we must be able to function and thrive even when our worlds are being turned upside down. We must know what God's Word says about our situations and trust in Him to lead and guide us when we do not know what to do.

18. How did your life begin? Was there something less than perfect surrounding your birth or in your early childhood? Explain.

_____
_____
_____
_____
_____
_____

19. Right now, do you feel your life is less than perfect? Explain.

_____
_____
_____
_____
_____

20. Do you blame someone for your life being less than perfect?

_____
_____
_____
_____
_____

21. What do you do when you do not know what to do?

_____
_____
_____
_____

22. What do you do when everything around you is in chaos?

_____
_____
_____
_____
_____

23. What do you do to maintain your sanity when life is less than perfect?

_____
_____
_____
_____

Since life is less than perfect, look up the following passages of scripture and write what each says to you. How can you apply them in your situation(s)?

1 Peter 5:7

_____
_____
_____

Philippians 4:19

_____
_____
_____

John 16:33

_____
_____
_____

Isaiah 26:3

_____
_____
_____

Matt 5:45

_____
_____
_____

1 Peter 4:12-13

Exercise ten

In the beginning: The making of woman

ଔ "When God made me, Woman, W-O-M-A-N, He had out done himself. I was Woman, W-O-M-A-N, God's final crowning act of creation. I was Woman, God's glorious masterpiece. I was the pinnacle of perfection on the day I was created. In fact, I was so fine and magnificent that God had no need to create anything else! So God rested from His labor. God indeed saved the best for last!"

(from *Coming Out of the Closet*, Chapter Ten)

As women, we may not fully understand the particular care, concern, and craftsmanship that God put into making us. When we grasp this, we will realize just how special we really are.

1. Where was Adam created? [Genesis 2:7]

___

2. On which day of creation was man formed? [Genesis 1:26, 27, 31]

___

3. On which day of creation was woman formed? [Genesis 1:27, 28, 31]

___

4. Where was she created? [Genesis 2:22]

___

5. What did God call them once they were created? [Genesis 5:1-2]

___

6. What were the differences between man's and woman's creation? [Genesis 2:7, 21, 22]

___

7. Why was woman created? [Genesis 2:18-20]

___

8. How was she created? [Genesis 2:21-23]

___

9. What was the environment like when woman was created? [Genesis 2:7]
___
___

10. What things contributed to the fall of woman? [Genesis 3]
___
___

11. What things contributed to the fall of man? [Genesis 3]
___
___

12. Are these problems still going on today for women? In what ways?
___
___

13. Are these problems still going on today for men? In what ways?
___
___

14. Why was the woman singled out first by Satan?
   a) ___
   ___
   b) ___
   ___
   c) ___
   ___
   d) ___
   ___

15. When did woman's name change? [Gen. 3:20]
___
___

16. What was woman's curse? [Genesis 3:10]
_____
_____

17. What can woman do to break these curses?
_____
_____

18. What was man's curse? [Genesis 3:17-20]
_____
_____

19. What can man do to break his curses?
_____
_____

20. What do you suppose happened to Adam and Eve's relationship after the fall?
_____
_____
_____
_____

21. What do you think Eve's life was like as a woman after the fall?
_____
_____
_____
_____

22. What do you think Adam's life was like after the fall?
_____
_____
_____

23. Whatever you think Eve's life was like after the fall, do you see any similarities in your life today, or in the life of wives, mothers, daughters, etc.? If so, what are the similarities?

_____
_____
_____
_____
_____
_____

24. Whatever you feel Adam's life was like after the fall, do you see any similarities in your life today, or in the life of your husband, son, father, etc.? If so, what are those similarities?

_____
_____
_____
_____
_____
_____

Exercise eleven
Issues, issues, issues

༄ One book cannot address all of the issues, situations, circumstances, trials, and conditions that cause women to find themselves locked in a closet. However, we must begin somewhere. Some of us have never dealt with these issues. While there are others who have acknowledged they have them, but they have yet to take the necessary measures to overcome them. Sadly, there are some who do not even realize the strongholds these issues can become.

(from *Coming Out of the Closet*, Chapter Eleven)

We all have issues! We all have struggled and are still struggling with some stronghold that hinders us from becoming who or what God created us to be. Let's begin to explore our issues. Write as detailed as possible, and take your time. This may be very difficult, but it is also very necessary. What you choose to share in a group setting is your choice. Let God lead you as to how much, when, and where. If you are suffering from any issues that make you physically, emotionally, and spiritually ill, **please seek counseling. Do not try to handle these issues on your own.**

Abortion

1. Have you been haunted by the issue of abortion? If not you, has someone you know?
_____
_____

2. How did it affect you or them?

Past effects:_____
_____
_____
_____
_____
_____
_____
_____
_____

Present effects:_____
_____
_____
_____
_____
_____
_____
_____

KEYS TO REMEMBER

Abortion
    I John 1:9
    Philippians 3:13-14

Abuse

3. Have you ever been a victim of abuse? Explain.

_____
_____
_____
_____
_____

4. How did it affect you?

_____
_____
_____
_____
_____

5. How is it affecting your present life (as an individual; as someone involved in a relationship)?

_____
_____
_____
_____
_____
_____
_____

KEYS TO REMEMBER

Abuse
Psalm 139:14
Joel 2:25

Anger

6. In your own words, define anger.

_____
_____
_____
_____

7. Are you angry? If so, why?

_____
_____
_____
_____
_____
_____
_____
_____

8. Does your anger stem from your past, present, or both?

_____
_____
_____
_____
_____
_____
_____
_____

9. If you do not feel you have an issue with anger, explain why. What advice can you offer to other women?

_____
_____
_____
_____
_____
_____
_____
_____

KEYS TO REMEMBER

Anger
   Mark 11:26
   Hebrews 10:30

Absent Father

10. Did you grow up with your father in your home?

11. If he was in the household, was he actively involved in your childhood?

12. Did your father teach you about the opposite sex? If not, who did? What impact did this have on you?

13. Did your father take you on your first date? Is this important to you? Explain.

14. If your father was in the home with you, what difference did it make in the choices you made in your life?

15. If your father was not in the home with you, what difference do you feel it has made in your life choices?

_____
_____
_____
_____
_____

16. Was your father emotionally involved in your life, or was he just there physically? What are your thoughts about the impact this has had or still has on your life?

_____
_____
_____
_____
_____
_____

17. How has your relationship, or lack thereof, with your father impacted how you have raised your daughter and/or your son?

_____
_____
_____
_____
_____

18. How has your relationship, or lack thereof, with your father impacted how you feel or have felt about yourself as a woman?

_____
_____
_____
_____
_____
_____

19. What has helped you hold it together while dealing with the issues you addressed in this lesson?

20. How do you perceive your future if these issues are not dealt with?

21. What resources do you need to help you?

22. If you have dealt with these issues, what is different about your present life?

23. How different is your future going to be because you have dealt with the issue(s)? What can you share with others to help them?

KEYS TO REMEMBER

Absent Father
    Psalm 68:5
    Hebrews 13:5

Exercise twelve

Take out the trash & throw away the garbage

Trash and garbage must be disposed of because they are not healthy for the person in possession of them or for the people who might be exposed to them. Traditionally, taking out the trash and throwing away the garbage has not been the woman's job. In our spiritual walk, however, if we want to live the abundant life that Jesus promised us, after accepting Christ as our personal Savior, we must begin the process of dumping the baggage owned by the old man (old sin nature).

(from *Coming Out of the Closet*, Chapter Twelve)

Many of us have been carrying around baggage, trunks, and dead weight for years. As a result, we have been so burdened and weighed down that, like our sister at the temple, we can in no wise lift up ourselves. We must begin to rid ourselves of these heavy weights, allow God to straighten us up, and then walk in FREEDOM!

Hebrews 12:1b-2a advises us to "lay aside every weight, and the sin which doth so easily beset us, and let us run with patience the race that is set before us, Looking unto Jesus, the author and finisher of our faith."

1. Are you the "Bag Lady," "Luggage Handler," or the "Trunk Toter"? Explain.

_____
_____
_____
_____

2. What have you been collecting? Are you still collecting?

_____
_____
_____
_____

3. Have you been able to empty anything out of your bag, luggage, or trunk? If so, what?

_____
_____
_____
_____

4. How have you been able to empty your load?

_____
_____
_____
_____
_____
_____
_____

If you have not been able to empty your load and need some guidance, in addition to getting involved in women's ministry, there is something you must do.

Step 1:	**A**cknowledge	Admit there is a problem.
Step 2:	**C**onfess	or S.T.R.I.P. (Stop to Reveal Internal Problems) What are those problems? What are your scars?
Step 3:	**T**rust God's Word	What does God's Word say about your issue(s)?
Step 4:	**S**tep out on faith	Stand on God's promise that He will, "after that ye have suffered a while, make you perfect, stablish, strengthen, settle you" (I Peter 5:10).

Find one of God's promises or instructions in His Word regarding the areas that still have you bound. Write it down and put it in an area where you can see it every day. Read it every day. Repeat it to yourself every day. Trust God's Word. Pray His Word (because **P**rayer **U**pholds, **S**ustains, and **H**eals). And finally, believe His Word!

When God's word comes off the pages of His Book and resides in our hearts, it will come alive. We will begin to walk in the light of His promise: walk by faith and not by sight. Day by day, our loads will become lighter. Our pasts will no longer haunt us and our futures will be bright. As we continue to "take out the trash and throw away the garbage," this is how we will move toward healing, wholeness, and freedom.

The old saying, "Guilt looks back, worry looks around, but faith looks up!" is very true. **A.C.T.** and then **S.**

Exercise Thirteen
FORGIVENESS

    Forgiveness is one of the basic tenets of Christianity. When we do not forgive, we are destroying ourselves physically, mentally, and spiritually. Unforgiveness is a debilitating and destructive prison. It destroys the person who refuses to forgive and often can destroy the one who is not forgiven. I teach the women in the ministry that forgiveness = freedom.

(from *Coming Out of the Closet*, Chapter Thirteen)

1. How would you define forgiveness?
   _____
   _____
   _____

2. There is a German proverb that says: "If it were not for God's forgiving grace, heaven would be empty." What does this mean to you?
   _____
   _____
   _____
   _____

Forgiveness of Others

3. Why is it so difficult to forgive others?
   _____
   _____
   _____
   _____

4. Mark 11:26 says, "But if ye do not forgive [others' trespasses], neither will your Father which is in heaven forgive your trespasses." What does this mean to you?
   _____
   _____
   _____

5. When we withhold forgiveness, who suffers more, us or the person who hurt us?
   _____
   _____
   _____

6. Is it possible to forgive someone without the person asking?
   _____
   _____

Forgiveness of Self

7. Is there something that has happened in your life for which you have not forgiven yourself?

8. Why is it so difficult to forgive yourself?

9. Jesus said in Matthew 12:31-32, "And so I tell you, every kind of sin and slander can be forgiven, but blasphemy against the Spirit will not be forgiven. Anyone who speaks a word against the Son of Man will be forgiven, but anyone who speaks against the Holy Spirit will not be forgiven, either in this age or in the age to come" (NIV). What is significant about this passage?

10. How does God see you? (Psalm 139:14; 1 Peter 2:9-10; Ephesians 4:32)

Forgiveness of God

11. Have you ever felt like God has forgotten you? What was the situation? Describe your feelings.

_____
_____
_____
_____
_____

12. Have you ever been angry with God or blamed Him for something (e.g., a failed relationship, the death of a loved one, financial stress, poor health)? Why?

_____
_____
_____
_____
_____

Let's look at Job. Job was a man who was called perfect and upright by God's own description (Job 1:1). He was blessed by God with a lovely family and a wealth of riches, cattle, and land. However, God allowed Satan to test Job. Satan was permitted to cause Job to be gravely ill and to take away everything Job had, but he was not allowed to touch his soul. Satan truly believed that once this was done, Job would turn on God, his Maker and Provider. Some might say Job had a right to be angry with God.

13. Read Job 14:14. What was Job's response?

_____
_____
_____
_____

In the midst of Job's love for God, perhaps his greatest struggle was dealing with the murmurings of his friends (Chapters 15-41). Job had to pray for his friends.

14. Read Job 42:10 & 12. What was the outcome for Job?

_____
_____

_____
_____

15. What lesson does this teach us?

_____
_____
_____
_____
_____
_____

EXERCISE FOURTEEN
I AM WHO GOD SAYS I AM

Before we can know who we are as women, we must first know who we are in Christ. The truth of the matter is that apart from Christ, we are nothing! We are not to be identified by the circumstances from whence we came but rather by the purpose for which we were born to fulfill. We no longer want to be defined by our painful past, our excruciating experiences, or the never-ending negative views of others, for we are who God says we are.

(from *Coming Out of the Closet*, Chapter Fourteen)

During our ongoing journey of becoming free from our closet experiences, we must know and fully embrace who and what we are in Christ. We must realize that we are not the sum total of those negative words people may have spoken to us or even those things that we may have done. We are who God says we are!

Isaiah 40:8 proclaims: "The grass whithereth, the flower fadeth: but the word of our God shall stand forever." Jesus is recorded in Matthew 24:35, Mark 13:31, and in Luke 21:33 as saying: "Heaven and earth shall pass away, but my words shall never pass away." Let us search the Scripture to find out exactly who we are in Christ.

Fill in the blanks (using the KJV).

1. I am _____ and _____ made. (Psalm 139:14)

2. But as many as received him, to them gave he _____ to become the _____ of _____. (John 1:12)

3. Therefore being _____ by _____. (Romans 5:1a)

4. We have _____ with _____ through our Lord Jesus Christ. (Romans 5:1b)

5. For if, when we were enemies, we were _____ to _____ by the death of his Son, much more, being _____, we shall be _____ _____ by His life. (Romans 5:10)

6. There is therefore now no _____ to them which are in Christ Jesus. (Romans 8:1)

7. Nay, in all these things we are _____ than _____ through him that loved us. (Romans 8:37)

8. If any man be in Christ, he is a _____ _____. (2 Corinthians 5:17a)

9. For he hath made him to be sin for us, who knew no sin; that we might be made the _____ of _____ in him. (2 Corinthians 5:21)

10. Christ hath _____ us from the _____ of the _____. (Galatians 3:13a)

11. Wherefore thou art no more a _____, but a son; and if a son, then an _____ of God through Christ. (Galatians 4:7)

12. According as he hath chosen us in him before the foundation of the world, that we should be _____ and without _____ before him in love. (Ephesians 1:4)

13. In whom we have _____ through his blood, the _____ of sins, according to the _____ of his grace. (Ephesians 1:7)

14. By _____ are ye _____ through faith; and that not of yourselves: it is the _____ of God. (Ephesians 2:8)

15. In whom we have _____ and _____ with _____ by the faith of him. (Ephesians 3:12)

16. And grieve not the holy Spirit of God, whereby ye are _____ unto the _____ of _____. (Ephesians 4:30)

17. In whom we have _____ through his _____, even the _____ of _____. (Colossians 1:14)

18. In the body of his flesh through death, to present you _____ and _____ and _____ in his sight. (Colossians 1:22)

19. Ye are _____ in _____, which is the head of all principality and power. (Colossians 2:10)

20. God hath not given us the _____ of fear; but of _____, and of _____, and of a _____ _____. (2 Timothy 1:7)

21. For by one offering he hath _____ for ever them that are _____. (Hebrews 10:14)

22. But ye are a _____ _____, a _____ _____, an _____ _____, a _____ _____. (1 Peter 2:9a)

23. According as his divine power hath _____ unto us _____ _____ that pertain unto _____ and _____, through the knowledge of him that hath called us to glory and virtue. (2 Peter 1:3)

24. If we confess our sins, he is faithful and just to _____ us our sins and to _____ us from all unrighteousness. (1 John 1:9)

25. Ye are of _____, little children, and have overcome them: because _____ is he that _____ _____ _____, than ____ that is in _____ _____. (1 John 4:4)

Can we lose our salvation? Explain based on Scripture.
_____
_____
_____
_____

Exercise Fifteen
Hands

> Ministry showed me that if I reached out to take the hand that offered freedom and healing, that touch would make me whole. Being touched by the hands of God is like no other touch we will ever experience. We may have been hurt at the hand of someone else, but the hand of Jesus can lift us from death to life.

(from Coming Out of the Closet, Chapter Fifteen)

1. Many weeks ago, you began this journey that, prayerfully, has helped you identify your "closet." Is there at least one area or situation that no longer weighs you down? If so, what is it?

2. Were there hands that touched you inappropriately? Explain.

3. How did that touch affect you (emotionally, physically, and spiritually)?

4. Do you feel the inappropriateness of that touch affected the choices you made as relates to men? If so, how? If not, what influenced your choices?

5. What are your thoughts about Venus de Milo?

6. When during your closet experience did you reach out for the touch of God? What made you realize you needed His touch?

_____
_____
_____
_____

7. How has the touch of God changed your life?

_____
_____
_____
_____

If you have not yet experienced the healing hands of God and feel you are still locked inside the prison of your closet, reach up right now and stretch your hands toward heaven. Cry out and tell God what you need. Tell Him that you have tried everything else to get through your unforgettable experience(s), but nothing has helped move you toward healing and wholeness. Go ahead. Give God a try. Let Him touch you with His healing hands of love!

I also encourage you to get involved in women's ministry. It is the next best answer to helping you **come out of the closet!**

BE BLESSED, MY SISTER

Notes

[1] Cynthia Hicks, *The Feminine Journey: Understanding the Biblical Stages of a Woman's Life* (Colorado Springs: NavPress, 1994).
[2] "Letters between Abigail Adams and Her Husband John Adams," The Liz Library, http://www.thelizlibrary.org/suffrage/abigail.htm.
[3] "Letters between Abigail Adams and Her Husband John Adams."